C000077894

HOLY**HABITS** BIBLE REFLECTIONS | GLADNESS AND GENEROSITY

The Bible Reading Fellowship
15 The Chambers, Vineyard
Abingdon OX14 3FE
brf.org.uk

The Bible Reading Fellowship (BRF) is a Registered Charity (233280)

ISBN 978 0 85746 837 6
First published 2020
10 9 8 7 6 5 4 3 2 1 0
All rights reserved

Text © individual authors 2020
This edition © The Bible Reading Fellowship 2020
Original design by morsebrowndesign.co.uk & penguinboy.net

The authors assert the moral right to be identified as the authors
of this work

Acknowledgements
Scripture quotations marked NRSV are taken from The New Revised
Standard Version of the Bible, Anglicised edition, copyright © 1989, 1995
by the Division of Christian Education of the National Council of the
Churches of Christ in the United States of America. Used by permission.
All rights reserved.

Scripture quotations marked NIV are taken from The Holy Bible, New
International Version (Anglicised edition) copyright © 1979, 1984, 2011
by Biblica. Used by permission of Hodder & Stoughton Publishers, a
Hachette UK company. All rights reserved. 'NIV' is a registered trademark
of Biblica. UK trademark number 1448790.

Scripture quotations marked NKJV are taken from the New King James
Version of the Bible copyright © 1979, 1980, 1982 by Thomas Nelson, Inc.
All rights reserved.

Every effort has been made to trace and contact copyright owners
for material used in this resource. We apologise for any inadvertent
omissions or errors, and would ask those concerned to contact us so that
full acknowledgement can be made in the future.

A catalogue record for this book is available from the British Library

Printed and bound in the UK by Zenith Media NP4 0DQ

GLADNESS AND GENEROSITY

BIBLE REFLECTIONS
40 READINGS AND REFLECTIONS

Edited by
ANDREW ROBERTS

Contents

Contents

Contents

| David Gilmore

About the writers

Steve Aisthorpe is the Church of Scotland's mission development worker for the Highlands and Islands. He was previously executive director of the International Nepal Fellowship and is the author of *The Invisible Church* (SAP, 2016). He loves being outdoors, whatever the weather, and is an enthusiastic coach and retreat leader.

Jo Swinney is an author, speaker and director of communications for CPO. She has written six books, most recently *Home: The quest to belong* (Hodder, 2017). She has an MA in theology from Regent College, Vancouver, and loves writing about the Bible. She lives with her family in Bath and blogs at **joswinney.com**.

David Spriggs is a Baptist minister who has also served with the Evangelical Alliance and Bible Society. He has written several books and until recently was commissioning editor for BRF's *Guidelines* Bible reading notes. In 'retirement', he is the minister of a church in Leicester.

David Gilmore is a husband, father and ordained elder of the United Methodist Church who serves as director of congregational development and revitalisation for the New York Conference. He is responsible for planting new churches; identifying, equipping and empowering emerging leaders; and supporting and nurturing the creation of new ministries.

Introduction to Holy Habits

> They devoted themselves to the apostles' teaching and fellowship, to the breaking of bread and the prayers. Awe came upon everyone, because many wonders and signs were being done by the apostles. All who believed were together and had all things in common; they would sell their possessions and goods and distribute the proceeds to all, as any had need. Day by day, as they spent much time together in the temple, they broke bread at home and ate their food with glad and generous hearts, praising God and having the goodwill of all the people. And day by day the Lord added to their number those who were being saved.
>
> ACTS 2:42–47 (NRSV)

Holy Habits is a way of forming disciples that is emerging anew from an exploration of this precious portion of scripture, Luke's famous portrait of the early church. As such, it is both deeply biblical and an approach that lives when infused with the life-giving breath of the Holy Spirit – the same Holy Spirit who brought life, energy and creativity to the first Christian communities.

Holy Habits is based upon a series of ten practices that are shown to be fruitful in the Acts 2 passage: biblical teaching, fellowship, breaking bread, prayer, sharing resources, serving, eating together, gladness and generosity, worship, and making more disciples. In this series of material, passages relating to the ten habits are explored one habit at a time, sometimes with reference to other habits. In real life, the habits all get mixed up and complement each other as part of a holistic way of discipleship. You may want to be alert to such connections.

There are many lists in the Bible, and with biblical lists the first and last items often have particular significance. In this list, it is significant that biblical teaching comes first. All of the habits are to be found throughout scripture, and healthy holy habits will be grounded in regular engagement with biblical teaching. This is a foundational habit.

The last habit is also significant. Commentators have remarked that it is no surprise that 'day by day the Lord added to their number' when life was lived in the way Luke describes. Many can be nervous of the word 'evangelism'. Holy Habits offers a way of being evangelistic that may help to assuage some of those nerves.

Holy Habits is a way of life for followers of Jesus individually and collectively. In Acts 2:42–47, Luke offers clues as to how these practices can be fruitful. Note the devotion he mentions at the beginning and the repeated use of the word 'all'. Holy Habits is a way of life for all ages (including children), cultures and contexts. The habits are to be lived day by day, in the whole of life, Monday to Saturday as well as Sunday. And note how Luke attributes the growth that results to the Lord. These are *holy* habits, which flourish when the Lord is at the centre of all.

Introduction to Gladness and Generosity

Gladness and Generosity is an interesting habit on which to reflect. It is one that takes us from the simple and everyday to the most profound matters of life and faith, from places of great joy to places of great pain.

As I write this piece, we are having a new boiler fitted. I actually quite like having tradespeople in and really enjoy plying them with drinks and biscuits. Today's engineer likes his coffee with one sugar and milk, and he's in luck today for the biscuits in stock are shortbread and chocolate digestives. It's a simple act of hospitality, but one that feels good and embodies the principles of this particular holy habit. Sometimes being glad and generous is about chocolate biscuits and parties and thank yous and laughter and seeing the smile of a child.

Sometimes it is much, much deeper. It is the joy of seeing a bright blue sky after coming through an operation. It is someone donating a kidney for a loved one. It is a Rwandan woman forgiving the man who butchered her brother during the genocide.

As the writers in this series remind us, gladness and generosity are signs of the kingdom and essential attributes of God's character. They are seen in the generosity of creation, with the accompanying sense of God's gladness when God sees that all that has been made is good. Generosity is encountered again in a very different way in the words of the Lord Jesus from the cross, 'Father, forgive them' (Luke 23:34, NRSV) and, 'Today you will be with me in Paradise' (Luke 23:43, NRSV).

It is not always easy to be glad and generous, and one of the gifts of another holy habit, fellowship, is the gift of people with whom we can be honest. People who can hold us when we are hurting, help us when we are struggling and pray for us when quite frankly we would rather be the polar opposites of glad and generous.

It is not always easy, but it is a habit, like all the other habits, to be practised and a way of life that our very divided world needs to rediscover. I was talking recently with a follower of Jesus who lives out his faith day by day as a professor of politics. As part of his work, he goes to countries recovering from often very vicious wars. A key part of the recovery process is gathering those who have been enemies around the generosity of a meal table. Exhausted with enmity, they discover a new gladness when they recognise each other's humanity and begin the slow process of forgiveness and reconciliation.

You and I may not be called upon to exercise gladness and generosity in such contexts, but we are called to practise this habit wherever we are set and whatever we do in our homes, communities, workplaces and churches. And don't forget the chocolate biscuits.

GLADNESS AND GENEROSITY

| Steve Aisthorpe

Awaking – and an awakening

Genesis 28:18–22

Early the next morning Jacob took the stone he had placed under his head and set it up as a pillar and poured oil on top of it. He called that place Bethel, though the city used to be called Luz. Then Jacob made a vow, saying, 'If God will be with me and will watch over me on this journey I am taking and will give me food to eat and clothes to wear so that I return safely to my father's household, then the Lord will be my God and this stone that I have set up as a pillar will be God's house, and of all that you give me I will give you a tenth.' (NIV)

| Steve Aisthorpe

Reflection

Jacob was a greedy cheat. Taking advantage of his brother's hunger, he snatched his birthright. Exploiting his father's frailty, he duped him into bestowing on him the blessing due to his brother. However, 60 miles into an arduous journey, such was his exhaustion that a rock for his head was all he required for a bed. Then, after a fitful sleep, waking from slumber became a spiritual awakening, as the significance of an astounding dream took hold.

Jacob was no pilgrim, earnestly pursuing God. He was no repentant prodigal, solemnly seeking forgiveness. The gracious God, however, did not wait for Jacob to perform an about-turn. God took the initiative: Jacob, alone and vulnerable, was promised the enduring presence of God; Jacob, the defenceless wanderer, was assured divine protection; Jacob, the covetous egotist, was cast in the ultimate drama, directed by none other than the creator of heaven and earth and performed for the benefit of all humankind.

Today's verses could sound like Jacob is engaged in brazen bargaining with the almighty; his offering could seem paltry. However, when read in context, we realise that Jacob is responding to overwhelming generosity with the most liberal response he can muster. By consecrating the stone, he determines that God's undeserved generosity will never be forgotten; in pledging 'a tenth' he commits to a lavish sacrifice, a symbolic dedication of everything to Yahweh-jireh, his provider.

Like Jacob, we too are a work in progress. Transformation occurs as we respond to his generosity. How might you do this today?

Steve Aisthorpe

When cruelty meets generosity

Genesis 45:8–11

' So then, it was not you who sent me here, but God. He made me father to Pharaoh, lord of his entire household and ruler of all Egypt. Now hurry back to my father and say to him, "This is what your son Joseph says: God has made me lord of all Egypt. Come down to me; don't delay. You shall live in the region of Goshen and be near me – you, your children and grandchildren, your flocks and herds, and all you have. I will provide for you there, because five years of famine are still to come. Otherwise you and your household and all who belong to you will become destitute."' (NIV)

| Steve Aisthorpe

Reflection

This passage provides a powerful commentary on one of the most remarkable narratives in literature. In the background are the flaws that so often poison human relationships: favouritism, jealousy and pride. As the experiences of Joseph illustrate so graphically, what can seem like trivial failings can become the roots of violence and serious social evils: one lie prompts another, one action sparks others. Like a snowball rolling downhill, a malevolent momentum develops.

The foolish immodesty of a 17-year-old prig, the one with the fancy coat and big dreams, provided fertile ground for everyday sibling rivalry to become acrimonious and bitter. Soon it mutated into festering resentfulness and inspired the plotting of cold-blooded murder and people trafficking. In fact, the whole backdrop for the account of Joseph and his brothers comprises the well-developed fruit of greed and envy: inequality, slavery, poverty and famine.

However, by the time we reach the scene in today's passage, God had performed major heart surgery on Joseph and guided circumstances to this remarkable example of God's providence. As the hideous horror of famine descended on the land of his upbringing, Joseph ascended to a position of unimaginable power. Such had been the depth of God's transformation of this man that, despite finding himself in the perfect position to exact an awful revenge, he recognised the long-term working of God's grace for the benefit of him, his family and the whole nation – and responded towards his persecutors in generosity.

> Gracious God, please help us to answer unkindness with generosity. Amen

| Steve Aisthorpe

The hallmark of true vision

Exodus 35:20–25

Then the whole Israelite community withdrew from Moses' presence, and everyone who was willing and whose heart moved them came and brought an offering to the Lord for the work on the tent of meeting, for all its service, and for the sacred garments. All who were willing, men and women alike, came and brought gold jewellery of all kinds: brooches, earrings, rings and ornaments. They all presented their gold as a wave offering to the Lord. Everyone who had blue, purple or scarlet yarn or fine linen, or goat hair, ram skins dyed red or other durable leather brought them. Those presenting an offering of silver or bronze brought it as an offering to the Lord, and everyone who had acacia wood for any part of the work brought it. Every skilled woman spun with her hands and brought what she had spun – blue, purple or scarlet yarn or fine linen.

(NIV)

| Steve Aisthorpe

Reflection

As Moses shared a vision for the tabernacle, a new focus for the community's worship, the Holy Spirit stirred the hearts of many people. Their joy-filled and generous giving demonstrated their commitment. Some provided materials. Others contributed their skills. Such was their response that Moses had to restrain their outpouring of generosity (Exodus 36:1–7).

In my work with churches, helping them develop a collective vision, I have become convinced that a key indicator of whether an idea is rooted in God's purposes is whether it stirs people to give and to get involved. An excellent idea may motivate enthusiasts, but it takes a God-given vision to inspire and mobilise the majority.

A friend recently told me about a church in which a woman placed her wedding ring in the offering. Asked about this, she explained how, considering Christ's ultimate offering for her, she wanted to give the most precious thing she owned. Although her offering was made in secret, the word got out and, as that story became known, a new spirit of generosity was awakened.

> The Sea of Galilee and the Dead Sea receive the same water, but whereas the former teems with life, the latter is barren. The River Jordon flows into the Sea of Galilee and out, down to the Dead Sea. The Dead Sea receives, but with no outflow, becomes lifeless.

| Steve Aisthorpe

Freely you have received, freely give

Deuteronomy 15:7–10

> If anyone is poor among your fellow Israelites in any of the towns of the land that the Lord your God is giving you, do not be hard-hearted or tight-fisted towards them. Rather, be open-handed and freely lend them whatever they need. Be careful not to harbour this wicked thought: 'The seventh year, the year for cancelling debts, is near,' so that you do not show ill will towards the needy among your fellow Israelites and give them nothing. They may then appeal to the Lord against you, and you will be found guilty of sin. Give generously to them and do so without a grudging heart; then because of this the Lord your God will bless you in all your work and in everything you put your hand to.
>
> (NIV)

| Steve Aisthorpe

Reflection

'Ideas worth spreading'. This is the mantra of TED, an organisation conceived to enable leaders in the fields of technology, entertainment and design (hence 'TED') to come together and share ideas. Nowadays, the impact of TED talks is immense as every day millions of people hear important ideas delivered in a pithy and powerful format.

Moses wrestled with the same challenge identified by the founders of TED: how to ensure that messages of crucial significance would be understood. Deuteronomy was his answer. Here is powerful, persuasive instruction on how to live intentionally as God's people in response to his love and mercy.

It is a masterclass in communication. Nobody could hear this sermon and not be utterly convinced of the absolute necessity of cultivating a habit of extreme generosity. Today's passage begins and ends with positive and unequivocal instructions to foster practices of liberal lending and generous giving. In between is a warning about the peril of ignoring his urging.

Moses hammers home the importance of gladness and generosity, piling one adverb on to another to emphasise the attitude the Lord longs to see: *freely* lend; *generously* give. The meanness of a heart of stone and a tightly clenched fist is contrasted with the compassionate humanity of an open hand offered to those in need.

> O Lord, our provider, all we are and all we have come from you. Grant us the love and courage to live a life of big-heartedness and open-handedness. Amen

| Steve Aisthorpe

Rejoice! It's a commandment

Deuteronomy 16:15–17

For seven days celebrate the festival to the Lord your God at the place the Lord will choose. For the Lord your God will bless you in all your harvest and in all the work of your hands, and your joy will be complete. Three times a year all your men must appear before the Lord your God at the place he will choose: at the Festival of Unleavened Bread, the Festival of Weeks and the Festival of Tabernacles. No one should appear before the Lord empty-handed: each of you must bring a gift in proportion to the way the Lord your God has blessed you. (NIV)

| Reflection |

God commands celebration! We are to make joy-filled acts of thanksgiving. Gladness and gratitude are indivisibly interwoven. The festivals mentioned in this passage celebrate both God's agricultural provision and his saving interventions.

The Festival of Unleavened Bread recalls when, following liberation from captivity, Israel ate the unrisen 'bread of affliction' (v. 3). This flat bread recollects their hasty departure and the Lord's later provision of manna, collected each morning, enough for each day – a survival strategy for weary Israelite travellers but also a foreshadowing of the 'the bread of life… come down from heaven' (John 6:35, 38). Moses urged the people to 'remember… never forget' (Deuteronomy 9:7); Christ, having shared bread and wine with his friends, implored them to 'do this in remembrance of me' (Luke 22:19).

The Festival of Weeks (Pentecost in Greek) is a harvest festival: 'Count seven weeks from the time you begin to put the sickle to the standing corn. Then celebrate… and rejoice' (Deuteronomy 16:9–11). For those of us whose source of food is a supermarket, it can be challenging to remember that 'daily bread' is the fruit of God's gracious provision. Moses urged the people to remember the Lord's generosity in the harvest, and Jesus commends us to pray, 'Give us today our daily bread' (Matthew 6:11).

The Festival of Tabernacles is a joy-fuelled thanksgiving for the final harvest and a conscious recalling of simple dwellings constructed after 40 years of rootless roving around Sinai – gratitude to a generous God for both a fruitful harvest and liberation from slavery.

> 'The Christian should be an alleluia from head to foot'
> (St Augustine).

| Steve Aisthorpe

Sleep on it!

Psalm 4:4–8

Be angry, and do not sin. Meditate within your heart on your bed, and be still. Offer the sacrifices of righteousness, and put your trust in the Lord. There are many who say, 'Who will show us any good?' Lord, lift up the light of Your countenance upon us. You have put gladness in my heart, more than in the season that their grain and wine increased. I will both lie down in peace, and sleep; for You alone, O Lord, make me dwell in safety.

(NKJV)

Reflection

The landscapes of our towns and cities have been transformed. A new architecture has sprung up to cultivate our consumption and to profit from our passion to possess. Crowds stream into 'cathedrals of consumption' to worship at the altar of consumerism. While David, the author of this psalm, would be shocked to see vast retail parks, his opening words (vv. 1–3) demonstrate that he was entirely familiar with the underlying values and assumptions that snare shopaholics and threaten to convince us that contentment can be bought.

The phrase 'be angry' literally means 'be agitated'. When we see people longing for contentment, peace and joy, but swept along by lies, we *should* be angry and agitated. But then David offers a strategy for coping: sleep on it! Be still and ensure that, through humble trust and simple obedience, we experience the light and warmth of the Lord's love and joy. Then, rather than being sucked in by the same deceptions, we will know profound peace. Instead of being discouraged by the naysayers so familiar to David, we will enjoy the security of God's grace. Far from being disheartened by the prosperity of those who appear to profit from choices that displease the Lord, our hearts will brim with the same gladness that inspired this psalm.

The final verse of today's passage is like the closing stanza of a lullaby. As we listen, confident of the presence of our loving God, we are assured of priceless contentment and ultimate security, available from one outlet only: 'You alone, O Lord, make me dwell in safety.'

> 'Watch out!... Life does not consist in an abundance of possessions' (Luke 12:15, NIV).

Steve Aisthorpe

The good shepherd

Psalm 23

The Lord is my shepherd, I lack nothing. He makes me lie down in green pastures, he leads me beside quiet waters, he refreshes my soul. He guides me along the right paths for his name's sake. Even though I walk through the darkest valley, I will fear no evil, for you are with me; your rod and your staff, they comfort me. You prepare a table before me in the presence of my enemies. You anoint my head with oil; my cup overflows. Surely your goodness and love will follow me all the days of my life, and I will dwell in the house of the Lord forever. (NIV)

Steve Aisthorpe

Reflection

A few years ago, after decades of excellent health, I plunged into a period of protracted illness. Like a roller coaster, swooping plunges into the depths were followed by painfully slow progress to regain previous levels, only to then be catapulted into the next gut-wrenching drop. Although I am normally an optimistic person, lengthy periods of chronic fatigue and lingering pain whittled away my resilience. During the deepest troughs, unable to read, there was a portion of scripture, one of the few I have managed to memorise, that brought encouragement and reassurance. This psalm was a well of assurance and an oasis of cheer while journeying through a desert of discouragement and despair.

The shepherds of David's world kept small flocks, harvesting wool over several years. They really did *lead* their sheep and they *knew* their sheep. A good shepherd enabled the flock to thrive by leading them to places of plentiful grazing, fresh water – and rest, untainted by fear of predators. David knew from experience the courage and commitment needed to be a good shepherd. He had killed bears and lions while protecting his father's sheep (1 Samuel 17:34–36). When Jesus said, 'I am the gate' (John 10:9), he had in mind the habit of the best shepherds to spend the night sleeping stretched across the entrance of the sheep fold, ensuring the safety and well-being of those under his charge in the most diligent and intimate way.

> Read again today's psalm, allowing the promises of provision, security, rest, guidance and hope to permeate the deepest parts of your being – and recognising the gladness that wells up in response.

| Steve Aisthorpe

Self-talk for the soul

Psalm 42:1–5

As the deer pants for streams of water, so my soul pants for you, my God. My soul thirsts for God, for the living God. When can I go and meet with God? My tears have been my food day and night, while people say to me all day long, 'Where is your God?' These things I remember as I pour out my soul: how I used to go to the house of God under the protection of the Mighty One with shouts of joy and praise among the festive throng. Why, my soul, are you downcast? Why so disturbed within me? Put your hope in God, for I will yet praise him, my Saviour and my God.

(NIV)

| Steve Aisthorpe

Reflection

Some psalms are outpourings of raw emotion. Using distilled, rich language, they paint a vivid portrait of our almighty creator. However, they also give us a language with which to speak *with* him. While they are words from God and about God, they also provide words to offer *to* God. They give us an extensive vocabulary of praise, grief, doubt, trust, anger, thanksgiving and much more.

The writer of Psalm 42 faced provocation and ridicule 'all day long'. The metaphors of thirst and hunger, powerful desires for essential human needs, express the depth of the narrator's longing for the living God. However, the constant taunts take a toll. Despondency and downheartedness wheedle their way into the soul, robbing us of God-given gladness.

The 16th-century theologian Ignatius of Loyola taught that life invariably includes seasons of 'consolation' (when we are keenly aware of God's love and activity) and 'desolation' (when God seems distant and doubt presses in). In times of desolation, we are tempted to turn inwards and slide into a spiral of negative thoughts. At such times, we need the wisdom of this psalm. We need to speak to our own soul, confronting discouragement and urging trust in God (vv. 5, 11). This is not mere positive thinking; it is choosing to take hold of God's promises. It is refusing to listen to ourselves and deciding to speak to ourselves instead.

> 'What, then, shall we say in response to these things? If God is for us, who can be against us?' (Romans 8:31).

| Steve Aisthorpe

Joy restored

Psalm 51:7–12

Cleanse me with hyssop, and I shall be clean; wash me, and I shall be whiter than snow. Let me hear joy and gladness; let the bones you have crushed rejoice. Hide your face from my sins and blot out all my iniquity. Create in me a pure heart, O God, and renew a steadfast spirit within me. Do not cast me from your presence or take your Holy Spirit from me. Restore to me the joy of your salvation and grant me a willing spirit, to sustain me.

(NIV)

| Steve Aisthorpe

Reflection

David was well acquainted with extreme gladness. Here was a man who danced with 'all his might', overwhelmed by pure delight in God's presence, as the ark of the covenant returned to Jerusalem (2 Samuel 6:14). David, trusted by God with immense power and responsibility, cast aside dignity and decorum as the joy of the Lord overwhelmed him.

However, David was also human. He was subject to the temptations that befall every man and woman, however devout. David, having allowed lust to find its toehold, found to his cost that the cascade into immorality can be steep and rapid. Failure to deal with lust led him into adultery. Then, desperate to keep his reputation intact, he tried to cover up his wrongdoing by abusing his power. Ultimately, he conspired to murder a faithful warrior and husband (2 Samuel 11).

What might it feel like to be a person of sincere devotion who then tumbles into such depths of immorality, corruption and violence? Well, Psalm 51 gives us a glimpse into the heart of David. When considered in the light of his previous faithfulness, we can appreciate the agonising pain in these words. David is crying out for forgiveness, cleansing and restoration. Entirely on the basis of God's 'unfailing love' and 'great compassion' (v. 1), without a shred of self-justification, David appeals to his creator. His intense longing is to be, once again, in right relationship with God. Then, and only then, might he be reacquainted with the joy of earlier times.

> David's experience shows us that joy, the fruit of God's Spirit, flourishes in the presence of righteousness, withers and dies in the face of rebellion, but can be restored by our gracious Saviour.

| Steve Aisthorpe

An uncontainable urge to worship

Psalm 100

> Shout for joy to the Lord, all the earth. Worship the Lord with gladness; come before him with joyful songs. Know that the Lord is God. It is he who made us, and we are his; we are his people, the sheep of his pasture. Enter his gates with thanksgiving and his courts with praise; give thanks to him and praise his name. For the Lord is good and his love endures forever; his faithfulness continues through all generations.
>
> (NIV)

| Steve Aisthorpe

Reflection

The author of this psalm is unidentified. However, we can be immensely grateful that not only did this person allow their gratitude to God to flood their soul with praise, but they also committed to writing the hymn of adoration and summons to worship that welled up in their heart. Then, fortunately for us, in the providence of God, more than five centuries before the birth of Christ, someone had the vision to collect together Hebrew poetry, including these precious words, into what comprises the book of Psalms, one of the most cherished books of the Bible.

Despite its ancient origin and the fact that some of its Hebrew poetic style is inevitably lost in translation, this poem speaks to us. It evokes in us the same overpowering riptide of thanksgiving that its author experienced. The same yearning to worship, felt by someone many centuries ago, is aroused in us. As the psalmist commands the whole of creation to turn to its maker in wholehearted praise, we too are caught up in what seems to be the only possible response. We just have to worship.

Packed into these verses we have a remarkably wide-ranging summary of the character of God, a surprisingly far-reaching synopsis of the relationship between God and his people, and an astonishingly helpful primer on how we should approach our creator. Recognising his awesome holiness and lavish generosity evokes in us a profound gladness, which overflows into worship, an unrestrained offering of our entire selves.

> Read Psalm 100 again, slowly. Pause after each instruction or statement and then respond in prayer before moving to the next. Like the psalmist, you may like to put your responses into writing.

GLADNESS AND GENEROSITY

| Jo Swinney

Why be generous?

Psalm 112:5–9

Good will come to those who are generous and lend freely, who conduct their affairs with justice. Surely the righteous will never be shaken; they will be remembered forever. They will have no fear of bad news; their hearts are steadfast, trusting in the Lord. Their hearts are secure, they will have no fear; in the end they will look in triumph on their foes. They have freely scattered their gifts to the poor, their righteousness endures forever; their horn will be lifted high in honour.

(NIV)

Reflection

Have you ever watched a televangelist in action? If you have, perhaps you were urged to 'sow a seed of blessing'. The idea is that if you give money to God (via this preacher and his TV ministry), this 'seed' will grow more money for you. Your generosity will be a wise financial investment.

Psalm 112:5 seems at first glance to be making that exact point: be generous and it will turn out well for you financially. Before we look more closely at what 'good' means here, though, it is worth noticing what is said about giving itself: it is equated with justice and righteousness. Whether or not we gain from it, it is right to be generous.

But the psalm says we do gain, if not in the ways we might think. So what is the 'good' that comes to the generous? First, they have a lasting legacy. They may not have a hospital or school named after them, but their memory will be kept alive. Second, they discover a freedom from fear and a faith in God that is a direct result of deciding not to hoard all their wealth for themselves. Money can't protect us from bad news, but for many of us it still gives a false sense of security. The cure for that is to scatter it around to those who need it. Whatever fundraising preachers may have us believe, giving away money doesn't make you richer – but it does result in righteousness, honour and freedom.

> Lord, help me be generous, because it is just and right, and because my true security is in you. Amen

| Jo Swinney

The wisdom of the giver

Proverbs 11:24–31

> One person gives freely, yet gains even more; another withholds unduly, but comes to poverty. A generous person will prosper; whoever refreshes others will be refreshed. People curse the one who hoards grain, but they pray God's blessing on the one who is willing to sell. Whoever seeks good finds favour, but evil comes to one who searches for it. Those who trust in their riches will fall, but the righteous will thrive like a green leaf. Whoever brings ruin on their family will inherit only wind, and the fool will be servant to the wise. The fruit of the righteous is a tree of life, and the one who is wise saves lives. If the righteous receive their due on earth, how much more the ungodly and the sinner!
>
> (NIV)

Reflection

The wise sayings in Proverbs are observations about what is, rather than promises for what will be. We might like to think that these verses are some kind of contractual statement from God about our bank accounts, but they aren't. They are statements about what generally happens in certain situations. People will like you if you give them stuff. If you bankrupt your parents, there won't be anything for you to inherit. It's all common sense if you think about it.

If there is a unifying theme in Proverbs, it is the question of how to live a good life. The answer is to seek wisdom, the source of which is God, and there is great wisdom in living generously. We live in a time and culture that encourages and even celebrates selfishness and greed. We are taught to look out for ourselves, save for our retirement, buy expensive insurance to cover every eventuality and put any spare cash into real estate or offshore savings accounts.

It may seem counter-intuitive, and it is certainly countercultural, but pouring out our resources on others is the way of wisdom. Generosity blesses the giver; it pleases God and it may well save lives along the way.

> Ask God to give you the wisdom to become
> more recklessly generous.

| Jo Swinney

The gladness of all creation

Isaiah 35:1–2, 5–6

The desert and the parched land will be glad; the wilderness will rejoice and blossom. Like the crocus, it will burst into bloom; it will rejoice greatly and shout for joy. The glory of Lebanon will be given to it, the splendour of Carmel and Sharon; they will see the glory of the Lord, the splendour of our God... Then will the eyes of the blind be opened and the ears of the deaf unstopped. Then will the lame leap like a deer, and the mute tongue shout for joy. Water will gush forth in the wilderness and streams in the desert.

(NIV)

| Jo Swinney

Reflection

The nation of Israel was weak and vulnerable in Isaiah's time, surrounded by enemies and often succumbing to the temptation to turn to human allies and false gods for help. Through Isaiah, God promises retribution on his chosen people's enemies; in chapter 34 Edom is in the firing line, but all their enemies are in trouble. Following the destruction of the enemy is a time of restoration, vividly pictured in today's passage.

One of the besetting sins of humanity is self-centredness. We often think in entirely anthropocentric terms when it comes to salvation. I'm sure most of us naturally focus on the healing of the blind, deaf, mute and lame in these verses. The hope of sight and hearing, freedom from pain, the ability to move and speak is a wonderful thing.

But the Bible speaks of God's love and concern for all creation. All creation bears the cost of the fall, 'groaning as in the pains of childbirth' (Romans 8:22), and all creation will celebrate as it is fully redeemed. It will 'be glad', 'rejoice and blossom', 'shout for joy'. The desert and the wilderness, places of dryness, desolation and death, will be once again fertile and well-watered. God loves and is glorified by the whole earth, and his intention is to rescue all things from death and decay. When we care for God's world, when we see its beauty and thank its maker, we make him glad.

> In what ways, large or small, could you participate in restoring gladness to a suffering corner of creation?

| Jo Swinney

Reclothed

Isaiah 61:1–3

The Spirit of the Sovereign Lord is on me, because the Lord has anointed me to proclaim good news to the poor. He has sent me to bind up the broken-hearted, to proclaim freedom for the captives and release from darkness for the prisoners, to proclaim the year of the Lord's favour and the day of vengeance of our God, to comfort all who mourn, and provide for those who grieve in Zion – to bestow on them a crown of beauty instead of ashes, the oil of joy instead of mourning, and a garment of praise instead of a spirit of despair. They will be called oaks of righteousness, a planting of the Lord for the display of his splendour. (NIV)

Reflection

There is so much pain in the world. The poor, the broken-hearted, the captives and the prisoners, those who mourn and grieve, the despairing: they are everywhere. They are us.

How can we possibly be glad in the face of all that hurts, all that is unjust, all that takes our courage and tramples it in the cold, hard light of reality? What is this good news that will set us free?

Seven centuries after the prophet Isaiah delivered his hopeful message, a man stood up in a synagogue in the town of Nazareth and proclaimed that this scripture had been fulfilled in their hearing. You can read about it in Luke 4. Jesus Christ is God's comfort to a broken world. His life, death and resurrection give all of us reason for hope and a source of joy.

Our gladness in the face of all that is wrong is a 'display of his splendour' – a testament to the spiritual gift of joy in God through the Spirit. During the times our emotions register no joy, gladness becomes a discipline, a spiritual practice. We have to choose to wear the crown of beauty and the garment of praise.

> Whether or not it matches your mood today, put on the garment of praise. Worship the God who is the source of all joy and comfort.

| Jo Swinney

Enabled to give

Malachi 3:9–12

'You are under a curse – your whole nation – because you are robbing me. Bring the whole tithe into the storehouse, that there may be food in my house. Test me in this,' says the Lord Almighty, 'and see if I will not throw open the floodgates of heaven and pour out so much blessing that there will not be room enough to store it. I will prevent pests from devouring your crops, and the vines in your fields will not drop their fruit before it is ripe,' says the Lord Almighty. 'Then all the nations will call you blessed, for yours will be a delightful land,' says the Lord Almighty.

(NIV)

| Jo Swinney

Reflection

My husband, Shawn, became a Christian when he was 17. He was raised by a drug-addicted single mother in the United States. The rules of social housing meant he had to move out at 18, so he lived in his car until he could afford to rent somewhere. Money was tight, but when he learnt about tithing, he promised God he'd give 10 per cent of every paycheck he received that summer to his church. After the first week he forgot, until a Sunday service at the start of September. He had no money left, but just then his mother – who had just begun joining him at church – handed him some mail that had come to her address. In it was a tax rebate for the exact amount he owed. He immediately wrote the cheque over to the church. It was a sign to him that God wanted to encourage his desire to be generous.

God's word here includes a threat and a promise. In holding back what was rightfully his, the Israelites were stealing from the almighty. Consider for a moment how outrageous that seems, and yet if we are honest I'm sure all of us have given less than we could have. We reap what we sow, and there are consequences for theft.

There is a promise, too. God challenges Israel to test him. If they bless others, he will pour out extravagant blessings on them, creating a beautiful virtuous circle of giving.

> Be sacrificially generous and ask God to enable you not only to survive but to be able to give even more.

| Jo Swinney

The blessed life

Matthew 5:3–12

'Blessed are the poor in spirit, for theirs is the kingdom of heaven. Blessed are those who mourn, for they will be comforted. Blessed are the meek, for they will inherit the earth. Blessed are those who hunger and thirst for righteousness, for they will be filled. Blessed are the merciful, for they will be shown mercy. Blessed are the pure in heart, for they will see God. Blessed are the peacemakers, for they will be called children of God. Blessed are those who are persecuted because of righteousness, for theirs is the kingdom of heaven. Blessed are you when people insult you, persecute you and falsely say all kinds of evil against you because of me. Rejoice and be glad, because great is your reward in heaven, for in the same way they persecuted the prophets who were before you.'

(NIV)

| Jo Swinney

Reflection

This teaching of Jesus is often called the beatitudes. Beatitude means blessedness and, taken together, these verses paint a picture of life in the kingdom of God. This picture is uncomfortable to contemplate, surprising and topsy-turvy, and yet more beautiful and compelling than any other vision of how life should be lived. All of it is framed in the perspective of what is to come. Jesus came from heaven and was returning to heaven, and he knew better than anyone that everything in-between was worth it.

Reading through this list, I'm sure like me you find some of the sayings more challenging than others. Perhaps you are naturally drawn to peacemaking but the word 'meek' makes your lip curl involuntarily. Jesus was the embodiment of the 'blessed' as depicted here, and, like it or not, this is what a Christlike life looks like. The insults, false accusations and persecution that result from true discipleship are signs we are on the right track and are therefore cause for rejoicing and gladness.

Father God, form me into the likeness of your Son Jesus. Thank you for the blessing of life in your kingdom. Amen

Jo Swinney

The gift of the kingdom

Matthew 10:5–11

These twelve Jesus sent out with the following instructions: 'Do not go among the Gentiles or enter any town of the Samaritans. Go rather to the lost sheep of Israel. As you go, proclaim this message: "The kingdom of heaven has come near." Heal those who are ill, raise the dead, cleanse those who have leprosy, drive out demons. Freely you have received; freely give. Do not get any gold or silver or copper to take with you in your belts – no bag for the journey or extra shirt or sandals or a staff, for the worker is worth his keep. Whatever town or village you enter, search there for some worthy person and stay at their house until you leave.'

(NIV)

Jo Swinney

Reflection

Jesus had a powerful and urgent message to deliver: 'the kingdom of heaven has come near.' He preached it; he reinforced it through miracles; his life was an embodiment of its truth. It was a message the whole world needed to hear: this kingdom was for anyone and everyone who heard, believed and repented, first the 'lost sheep of Israel' and then the rest of us (Matthew 28:19). Those in the kingdom would live forever, at peace with God.

For the three years leading up to his death, Jesus was constantly on the road – drawing crowds on hillsides, in homes and in synagogues. But while he was God, he was also a man and therefore constrained by the limits of time and space. This commission to his closest twelve followers was a response to the need: 'the harvest is plentiful but the workers are few' (Matthew 9:37). He needed to delegate.

The responsibility for announcing the kingdom of God is now for all of its citizens. We have been given, most extravagantly, the generous gifts of life, belonging and connection. The most generous thing we can do is to make sure we shout about it from the rooftops.

Who is waiting to be invited into the kingdom of God? It may not be the obvious people. Ask the Holy Spirit to give you the words to speak and his compassion for the lost.

Joyful generosity

Matthew 19:21–24

> Jesus answered, 'If you want to be perfect, go, sell your possessions and give to the poor, and you will have treasure in heaven. Then come, follow me.' When the young man heard this, he went away sad, because he had great wealth. Then Jesus said to his disciples, 'Truly I tell you, it is hard for someone who is rich to enter the kingdom of heaven. Again I tell you, it is easier for a camel to go through the eye of a needle than for someone who is rich to enter the kingdom of God.'
>
> (NIV)

Reflection

Chuck Feeney is an Irish-American businessman who has made a fortune in duty-free shopping. He lives in a rented apartment, travels economy class and to date has given away over $8 billion. In a letter to fellow philanthropist Bill Gates, he explained, 'The process of – and most importantly, the results from – granting this wealth to good causes has been a rich source of joy and satisfaction to me and for my family.'

Humans have always been susceptible to idol worship – investing value and worth in inappropriate places. It is so easy to fall for the lie that possessions will make us happy, safe and powerful. That is why Jesus seems harsh and unreasonable in this exchange with the rich young man. How could anyone even consider giving everything away?

What Jesus knew, and what Chuck Feeney knows, is that radical generosity is the key that buys our freedom. There is real, true, priceless treasure in heaven. It is worth more than anything our grubby mitts can grasp on to. And it is ours for the taking once we stop hoarding and start giving.

> Lord God, I am sorry for undervaluing heavenly treasure and investing in the wrong kind of wealth. Help me to trust your judgement on what matters and to bless others with what I have. Amen

Jo Swinney

Kingdom asset management

Matthew 25:24–28

(Then the man who had received one bag of gold came. "Master," he said, "I knew that you are a hard man, harvesting where you have not sown and gathering where you have not scattered seed. So I was afraid and went out and hid your gold in the ground. See, here is what belongs to you." His master replied, "You wicked, lazy servant! So you knew that I harvest where I have not sown and gather where I have not scattered seed? Well then, you should have put my money on deposit with the bankers, so that when I returned I would have received it back with interest. So take the bag of gold from him and give it to the one who has ten bags."'

(NIV)

| Jo Swinney

Reflection

Jesus often taught by telling stories, known as parables. In this parable, a man goes travelling and leaves his wealth in the hands of three servants. On his return, two of them have invested the gold and their investment has paid dividends – they are able to give the man more than he left them with. The third man buries his gold in the ground. He doesn't lose it, but he has wasted its worth, which he could have leveraged to generate more.

In essence, this is a story about stewardship. God is the ultimate owner of all that we have – not just our money, but our time, abilities and skills. As the three servants have differing quantities of gold at the outset, so we have varying assets. What is true for all of us, however, is the potential to invest what we're given wisely so that it grows.

The reason the one-bag-of-gold-servant gives for refusing to do anything with his portion was that he didn't want the master to gain (harvesting a crop he didn't sow himself). By implication, when we are good stewards of what we have, all benefit is God's. What better motivation to make the very most of our assets, investing them where they will give glory to our heavenly Father?

Do a quick audit of the 'gold' God has entrusted to you. How can you most effectively invest it in growing God's kingdom?

| Jo Swinney

Reasons to be glad

Luke 1:46–55

And Mary said: 'My soul glorifies the Lord and my spirit rejoices in God my Saviour, for he has been mindful of the humble state of his servant. From now on all generations will call me blessed, for the Mighty One has done great things for me – holy is his name. His mercy extends to those who fear him, from generation to generation. He has performed mighty deeds with his arm; he has scattered those who are proud in their inmost thoughts. He has brought down rulers from their thrones but has lifted up the humble. He has filled the hungry with good things but has sent the rich away empty. He has helped his servant Israel, remembering to be merciful to Abraham and his descendants forever, just as he promised our ancestors.' (NIV)

| Jo Swinney

Reflection

Scholars believe Mary was a young teenager when her life was turned upside down by an unexpected pregnancy. Her arrangement with Joseph was more than an equivalent to today's engagement; the commitment involved was not far short of marriage. It was potentially devastating to risk a betrothal. Mary knew the baby was God's own Son, but she also knew it would be hard convincing anyone else of that. You might think she'd be praying something along the lines of 'Oh Lord, why did you get me in this mess? Please make my life easier.' But here she is, full of joy and gratitude, her entire focus on God's blessing and favour.

A Chinese pastor was sent to a prison camp, where he spent 18 years. Under constant observation, Pastor Chen prayed for space to worship God, pray and speak out scripture. One day he was assigned to scoop out human waste from the cesspool for fertiliser. No one went near the cesspool because of the stench and risk of disease. Pastor Chen spent the next six years using his hours in this hell on earth to praise God at the top of his voice.

However terrible our circumstances, as followers of Christ we have reasons for gladness. God is our merciful saviour. He has performed mighty deeds. He keeps his promises.

> Pray Mary's prayer and ask God to remind you of the many reasons he has given you to be glad.

| David Spriggs

Generosity: a sign of the kingdom

Luke 3:10–14

'What hat should we do then?' the crowd asked. John answered, 'Anyone who has two shirts should share with the one who has none, and anyone who has food should do the same.' Even tax collectors came to be baptised. 'Teacher,' they asked, 'what should we do?' 'Don't collect any more than you are required to,' he told them. Then some soldiers asked him, 'And what should we do?' He replied, 'Don't extort money and don't accuse people falsely – be content with your pay.' (NIV)

David Spriggs

Reflection

It had been like waiting at temporary traffic lights for ages. You begin to wonder if they will ever change and you can get moving again. Only, in this case, it *had* been ages: approximately 400 years of hopes followed by bitter disappointments, as God's people waited for the one who would prepare the way for his Messiah, fill in the potholes and make the highway straight and safe.

Now, it seemed, he was here. A big part of that preparation was calling people to repentance, a fundamental change of mind, so that God and his ways came first. This change of mind involved a complete and radical reorientation of their lives.

Three different types of people are mentioned here. At first sight, the required changes seem somewhat random. Soldiers are to stop grumbling about their pay and refrain from using their power to demand extra money. Tax collectors normally made their money by adding on extra to their invoices, over and above what the Romans would demand from them. John the Baptist said that had to stop. As for ordinary people, if they had an extra shirt, they were to give it away to someone more needy, and if they had any spare food they were to hand it out to people who had none.

What's the common thread? It is about centring on God and therefore being content and secure, because if we are secure we can become generous. Positively, we can give away anything over to those more needy than us and we can abstain from grasping what we can get from others because of our power. Generosity is a sign of the coming kingdom.

> Consider the connection between feeling secure
> and being generous, in your experience.

| David Spriggs

Overflowing generosity

Luke 6:35–38

'But love your enemies, do good to them, and lend to them without expecting to get anything back. Then your reward will be great, and you will be children of the Most High, because he is kind to the ungrateful and wicked. Be merciful, just as your Father is merciful. Do not judge, and you will not be judged. Do not condemn, and you will not be condemned. Forgive, and you will be forgiven. Give, and it will be given to you. A good measure, pressed down, shaken together and running over, will be poured into your lap. For with the measure you use, it will be measured to you.'

(NIV)

| David Spriggs

Reflection

Generosity is the overflowing of God's heart. God's generosity is like a large waterfall. As the onrushing water reaches the waterfall's edge, it cascades and tumbles over. It falls and splashes anywhere and everywhere. It doesn't flow in an orderly straight line and through constructed channels. It's as though the water has been freed. Delighting in its freedom, it runs wild, bouncing and foaming as it hits rocks, splashing and spraying in every direction. Then, when the sun shines, a beautiful rainbow appears through the spray, celebrating its unfettered spirit. Such, says Jesus, is the generosity of God.

Over Christmas, I was given some bottles of good-quality grape juice – not just a couple of bottles but a box of twelve. Overflowing generosity! It was a heart-warming experience, all the more so because it was unexpected and unearned. This meant that I could be generous in return, giving some bottles to others and ensuring that our guests had ample supplies.

Jesus indicates several features of God's generosity. He gives without any expectation or impression that he expects to be paid back. He is kind. He is merciful, that is, he doesn't react to the damage people do by punishment or by withholding his generosity. He gives more than is necessary or expected. But if we want to experience this kind of generosity, then we also need to practise it.

Think of times when you have been the recipient of other people's generosity. How did it make you feel towards them? How did it make you feel personally? When can you put this habit into practice?

| David Spriggs

The wellspring of joy

Luke 10:17–21a

The seventy-two returned with joy and said, 'Lord, even the demons submit to us in your name.' He replied, 'I saw Satan fall like lightning from heaven. I have given you authority to trample on snakes and scorpions and to overcome all the power of the enemy; nothing will harm you. However, do not rejoice that the spirits submit to you, but rejoice that your names are written in heaven.' At that time Jesus, full of joy through the Holy Spirit, said, 'I praise you, Father, Lord of heaven and earth.'

(NIV)

| David Spriggs

Reflection

Four times in this short passage the words 'joy' or 'rejoicing' occur. Being joyful is often the wellspring for a 'glad and generous heart'.

I wonder what it was that made the disciples joyful when they returned. I sense four things may have contributed to this. First, they were back with Jesus. There is usually a sense of joy when we get back home safely. Even after a great holiday, while I may be reluctant to leave, there is still a joy in returning home to familiar things and to people I love. How much more must this have been true for the disciples after their arduous mission.

Then, they had good news to report. 'Even the demons submit to us in your name,' they announced. There had been success on their mission. Achievements, especially those involving risks, bring with them a sense of fulfilment, satisfaction and joy.

Third, I discern the joy of the unexpectedly good. When they say 'even', it implies that this was the pinnacle of the challenge (better than preaching or healing) and even that had come about. It surpassed their expectations. Imagine a teenager, hoping for a B grade to qualify for university, who finds out on results day that they have an A*. Anxiety is banished by the joy of unexpected success.

Finally, there was the joy of seeing lives transformed, as the grip of Satan that had distorted people's personalities and behaviour was broken.

Surely that is enough! Oh no, says Jesus. Even greater than kingdom success is your privilege of belonging to God, in time and eternity.

> Pray for the joy of kingdom success in your church.
> Praise God that you belong to him.

David Spriggs

Always glad and generous?

Luke 10:30, 33–35

> In reply Jesus said: 'A man was going down from Jerusalem to Jericho, when he was attacked by robbers. They stripped him of his clothes, beat him and went away, leaving him half-dead... But a Samaritan, as he travelled, came where the man was; and when he saw him, he took pity on him. He went to him and bandaged his wounds, pouring on oil and wine. Then he put the man on his own donkey, brought him to an inn and took care of him. The next day he took out two denarii and gave them to the innkeeper. "Look after him," he said, "and when I return, I will reimburse you for any extra expense you may have."'
>
> (NIV)

| David Spriggs

'Glad and generous hearts'? I wonder if that is how the Samaritan felt when he saw the writhing mess of humanity lying across his path as he made his way home. He probably felt anxious, lest he should be attacked by the robbers he had heard were around.

I don't always feel glad and generous when my plans are interrupted by a plea for help on the phone or by a request to go and childmind. It's natural to feel a degree of annoyance. But the Samaritan's 'glad and generous' heart is shown by his practical response. He didn't avoid the obvious challenge, as the priest and Levite had done; he went and took a good look, examined him and then he had compassion for him. This led to the traveller not only taking remedial first aid action but going way beyond what could be expected by ensuring that the injured man was looked after in a safe place that night. His generosity is shown by his open-ended provision for the man's needs – the equivalent of leaving the innkeeper with your debit card!

From time to time, needy people make their way into our churches, both during service times and on other occasions. How we treat such people will say a lot about just how 'glad and generous' we are that God has rescued us, bathed us in his love and renewed us.

> Think about someone who comes to your church and consider how you could be more generous in your attitudes and actions.

| David Spriggs

A father's generosity

Luke 15:20–24

'So he got up and went to his father. But while he was still a long way off, his father saw him and was filled with compassion for him; he ran to his son, threw his arms round him and kissed him. The son said to him, "Father, I have sinned against heaven and against you. I am no longer worthy to be called your son." But the father said to his servants, "Quick! Bring the best robe and put it on him. Put a ring on his finger and sandals on his feet. Bring the fattened calf and kill it. Let's have a feast and celebrate. For this son of mine was dead and is alive again; he was lost and is found." So they began to celebrate.' (NIV)

| David Spriggs

This father had every right to be bitter and hard-hearted. For many months at least, he had had to cope without the labour of his wayward son. Every night, he could have bemoaned the fact that his son had been so ungrateful and was wasting the resources he had worked so hard to build up. Being treated like that can twist your soul; similar abysmal behaviour from a work colleague or friend, let alone our own flesh and blood, can be a corrosive turning us into a bitter person.

But love conquers everything! To the father, his son mattered more than property or possessions. His love for his son was stronger than the insult and offence his son had caused him. The father's generous and forgiving nature had not been diminished by the comments or the pain. So it was as soon as he glimpsed his son from far away that generosity kicked into gear and he was running down the dusty path to greet him. All caution was thrown to the wind (Was his son 'unclean'? Would he be contaminated? What would his neighbours think?), as he threw his arms round him, hugged him and kissed him.

His joy at his son's return mixed with his natural generosity. Without hesitation or calculation, he ordered a magnificent night of celebration and made it clear that his son was welcome back and, indeed, was the guest of honour.

> How do you think the father's total acceptance impacted the son?

61

Generosity spreading blessings far and wide

Luke 19:5–9

When Jesus reached the spot, he looked up and said to him, 'Zacchaeus, come down immediately. I must stay at your house today.' So he came down at once and welcomed him gladly. All the people saw this and began to mutter, 'He has gone to be the guest of a sinner.' But Zacchaeus stood up and said to the Lord, 'Look, Lord! Here and now I give half of my possessions to the poor, and if I have cheated anybody out of anything, I will pay back four times the amount.' Jesus said to him, 'Today salvation has come to this house, because this man, too, is a son of Abraham.' (NIV)

| David Spriggs

Reflection

In the previous reading, the prodigal's father showed his glad and generous heart by unexpectedly welcoming his son. Here, Zacchaeus' glad and generous heart is triggered when he is unexpectedly welcomed by Jesus. God's offer of unconditional love and unwarranted forgiveness has tremendous power to release in us the same qualities that we have received.

Hence Zacchaeus 'came down at once and welcomed him gladly'. Some people can feel almost as glad when the vicar remembers their name and speaks to them at the door; others, because they are surprised that they are allowed to come to church in jeans. For Zacchaeus, Jesus' offer to come to his house to eat with him blew him away.

There was nothing in the world that could have meant more to Zacchaeus. He did not need physical healing for himself or any family member; he did not have a theological question he needed solving by this brilliant young rabbi; he did not need feeding in a desert place. He needed to know God loved him. That's what Jesus' affirming words and actions conveyed.

It was not long before Zacchaeus' gladness transmuted into generosity. His experience of Jesus set him free: free to admit he had cheated others; free, too, to become Jericho's leading philanthropist.

This is one of the wonderful things about generosity – it can spread the blessing far and wide. There would be many households in Jericho that night who could afford wine and good food to celebrate because Zacchaeus was free to give.

> What steps will you take to express to others God's amazing love for you?

David Spriggs

God's measures

Luke 21:1–4

As Jesus looked up, he saw the rich putting their gifts into the temple treasury. He also saw a poor widow put in two very small copper coins. 'Truly I tell you,' he said, 'this poor widow has put in more than all the others. All these people gave their gifts out of their wealth; but she out of her poverty put in all she had to live on.'

(NIV)

Reflection

The disciples, we are told, were coping with fear and anxiety – they knew their lives were at risk. In the last couple of days, they had seen Jesus snatched by temple guards, then tortured and brutally murdered by the Romans. They might well be next. It wasn't a pleasant thought. But they would also recall what fear had done to them during these terrifying events. When the guards came for Jesus, they had fled. When he was being tried and tortured, one of them had denied being associated with Jesus. Then when he was crucified, they had kept their distance so they wouldn't be arrested. Fear is a destructive and demoralising force. Maybe they were also fearful that if the rumours were true and Jesus were alive, he would banish them from his presence – 'Those who deny me, I will deny,' he had said.

What a shock, then, when suddenly Jesus is standing in front of them. But there was no recrimination or rejection; instead, they received the reassurance that it was him – the wounds were still there. Then the offer of 'peace': the relationship was re-established. Next, there would be the challenge to offer to others the same gracious forgiveness he had given them.

When anyone who feels they have failed themselves and God discovers through words of kindness and acceptance that God's love is real and is really available for them, what relief and joy is theirs. But their joy is also a gift to the one sharing God's love with them.

> Pray for those (including yourself) who need to experience Jesus' releasing forgiveness, peace and consequent joy. Is there anyone you need to forgive today?

| David Spriggs

Be generous with what you have

Acts 3:6–7, 9–10

Then Peter said, 'Silver or gold I do not have, but what I do have I give you. In the name of Jesus Christ of Nazareth, walk.' Taking him by the right hand, he helped him up, and instantly the man's feet and ankles became strong... When all the people saw him walking and praising God, they recognised him as the same man who used to sit begging at the temple gate called Beautiful, and they were filled with wonder and amazement at what had happened to him.

(NIV)

Reflection

How can we be generous when we don't have enough for ourselves? Peter shows a great attitude: he thinks of what he does have, not what he doesn't. It is important to be honest with ourselves and others about our limitations. He tells the man that he can't respond as the man hoped, as he doesn't have money. Peter could have bemoaned the fact that as a disciple he doesn't have as much money as he once had as a full-time fisherman. He doesn't drift into nostalgia, nor does he feel embarrassed about this. Rather, he utilises what he knows he does have. So he takes the risk of offering this man healing in Jesus' name.

As churches, we can bemoan the fact that we don't have parents with children or young people to look after and to share the faith with. A church I know was in this position. They realised, however, that they had a grassy area running down the side of the building and that there were many children living on the estate around them. So they hired two donkeys on the day before Palm Sunday and gave free donkey rides to the children on this lawn. They provided drinks for the parents and craft activities about Palm Sunday, Good Friday and Easter Sunday for everyone, so they could share the good news with all who came. They now have a prayer tent and offer prayer for healing. Their Messy Church can have up to 40 children turning up.

> Think about your opportunities, and pray that God
> will show you how to use them.

GLADNESS AND GENEROSITY

| David Gilmore

The power of one

Acts 4:32–35

Now the whole group of those who believed were of one heart and soul, and no one claimed private ownership of any possessions, but everything they owned was held in common. With great power the apostles gave their testimony to the resurrection of the Lord Jesus, and great grace was upon them all. There was not a needy person among them, for as many as owned lands or houses sold them and brought the proceeds of what was sold. They laid it at the apostles' feet, and it was distributed to each as any had need.

(NRSV)

Reflection

I am the product of a giving grandmother. I grew up witnessing a little lady who did not possess much make place for people in need. What made these acts of generosity even more amazing was the gladness with which my grandmother gave. She did not have much in the way of material resources, but she gave with her whole heart willingly and gladly to her church, her neighbours and her family.

What kind of community would we be part of if we tried the same thing? How many hungry mouths would be fed? How many homeless 'saints' would be sheltered? How many of our elderly and children would be spared lonely existences? I believe that in order to change a thing, we must become part of that thing. In order to share the love of Jesus, we must be willing to share those things our Lord Jesus has placed in our care.

And it all begins with the power of one! One faith community – like that described by Luke in our passage – can determine to embody the life and love of Jesus, sharing what we have with society's have-nots and changing our world one community at a time. One faith community can allow themselves to remember that our greatest witness to a heart-warming, soul-stirring, life-changing encounter with the resurrected Christ comes not solely from our mouths, but more importantly in our engagement with the least, last and lost in and of our world.

We have what we have and are who we are because of the immeasurable grace of our Lord Jesus, who gave of himself with a glad heart and willing spirit, with no strings attached. We give because he gave. We give because Jesus showed us how to give. We give, with gladness and generosity.

Lord, may the fellowship of which I am part be of one heart and mind in caring for those you love.

David Gilmore

Shaken and stirred

Acts 16:25–34 (abridged)

About midnight Paul and Silas were praying and singing hymns to God... Suddenly there was an earthquake, so violent that the foundations of the prison were shaken; and immediately all the doors were opened and everyone's chains were unfastened. When the jailer woke up and saw the prison doors wide open, he drew his sword and was about to kill himself.... But Paul shouted in a loud voice, 'Do not harm yourself, for we are all here.' The jailer called for lights, and rushing in, he fell down trembling before Paul and Silas. Then he brought them outside and said, 'Sirs, what must I do to be saved?' They answered, 'Believe on the Lord Jesus, and you will be saved, you and your household.' They spoke the world of the Lord to him and to all who were in his house. At the same hour of the night he took them and washed their wounds; then he and his entire family were baptised without delay. He brought them up into the house and set food before them; and he and his entire household rejoiced that he had become a believer in God.

(NRSV)

David Gilmore

Reflection

I am a fan of James Bond movies. I grew up loving the fast cars, unbelievable gadgets and continual danger constantly surrounding Agent 007. I remember all the different Bond actors – one line they all have in common is when Bond orders his favourite libation: 'shaken not stirred'.

In our reading, the jailer has been shaken and stirred. The idea that he may have lost the prisoners has him so distraught that he sees suicide as his salvation. Yet, the one who has been jailed offers real hope, real salvation, to the jailer. This unbelievable act of generosity on the part of Paul leads to new life not only for the oppressor, but also for his family. How might our world be changed if we remembered to see *all* of God's family as just that… God's family? How might the 'chains' of addiction and abuse and heartache and loneliness and hopelessness be broken if we but offer a word of grace, believing that that word has the power to change any one and anything?

The glad sharing of the good news leads to a stirring transformation in the jailer, evidenced in his generous offering of medical treatment and food. But it goes much deeper! Paul and Silas' sharing leads to a glad response by the jailer and his entire household. Their generous spirits, despite their physical circumstances, lead to a transformation no one could have foreseen.

Lord, shake and stir me to be an agent of your salvation.

David Gilmore

Could you? Would you?

Acts 20:32–35

' And now I commend you to God and to the message of his grace, a message that is able to build you up and to give you the inheritance among all who are sanctified. I coveted no one's silver or gold or clothing. You know for yourselves that I worked with my own hands to support myself and my companions. In all this I have given you an example that by such work we must support the weak, remembering the words of the Lord Jesus, for he himself said, "It is more blessed to give than to receive."' (NRSV)

| David Gilmore

Reflection

I offer this reflection with the caveat that I am an ordained minister of the gospel compensated by my church. As long as I have been appointed to serve the church, I have received some semblance of compensation. While I am grateful for the financial support I receive from my church, what brings me the greatest joy is engaging in the life of my neighbourhood and the lives of my neighbours, and being both transformed and transformational. I love being part of a movement that reminds my neighbours that they are worthy and not worthless, treasured and not trash. The world does a great job of minimising our marginalised sisters and brothers. The world seems to find delight in keeping the least least, the last last and the lost lost.

Maybe if we interacted with those who may be deemed 'weak', mindful that we were, are and/or will be weak too, we might possess an empathy that allowed us to give beyond what makes us comfortable with real joy, which might manifest an indescribable love to those the world has ostracised. It is in the hope-filled eyes of our sisters and brothers that we see the hope for ourselves, and hopefully will hear one day, 'Well done, good and faithful servant' (Matthew 25:23, NIV).

Could you give with no expectation of receiving? Would you give knowing there is nothing compensatory returning to you? Would you be willing to roll up your sleeves to engage in a work that restores dignity to those who are constantly reminded, 'You are less than'? There is no amount of gold or silver or clothing that elicits the same joy as witnessing a transformed heart!

> Lord, thank you that when we bless by giving of ourselves gladly and generously, we gain a reward that is greater than silver or gold.

| David Gilmore

Hope in the present

1 Corinthians 1:4–9

I give thanks to my God always for you because of the grace of God that has been given you in Christ Jesus, for in every way you have been enriched in him, in speech and knowledge of every kind – just as the testimony of Christ has been strengthened among you – so that you are not lacking in any spiritual gift as you wait for the revealing of our Lord Jesus Christ. He will also strengthen you to the end, so that you may be blameless on the day of our Lord Jesus Christ. God is faithful; by him you were called into the fellowship of his Son, Jesus Christ our Lord.

(NRSV)

| David Gilmore

Reflection

What's going on in your part of the world? It appears that on whichever part of the globe we reside, something *wrong* is happening. Whether it's the Brexit fight in the UK, cyclones in Mozambique or how disunited the United States is socially, politically and ecclesiastically – *something* wrong is happening.

Times like these are not for the faint-hearted. It seems that we cannot have a disagreement without becoming disagreeable or a discussion without becoming disgusting. Even within the body of Christ, there is tension and turmoil. In my denomination, the United Methodist Church, we are fighting among ourselves over the issue of human sexuality, while it seems that millennials and post-millennials are running away from any semblance of church.

Yet, in the midst of our squabbling, I still have hope, because I believe that God has prepared the church for such a time as this. I witness the explosion of the Fresh Expressions movement, here and abroad, and believe we are experiencing a rebirth of the church. There is a movement of the Spirit occurring within many of the mainline denominations that hearken back to Jesus' commandment to make disciples, baptise, teach and remember (Matthew 28:19–20).

There is hope in the present and a reason for real joy, because the timeless grace of God covers us before we realise we're covered; and the justifying grace of Jesus forgives, reconciles and restores us to right relationship with God; and the sanctifying grace of the Holy Spirit continually transforms us in order that we might remain in right relationship with God.

Yes, we, whose faith lies in Christ Jesus, have a reason to rejoice today, as Paul rejoiced in our passage, writing to a fractious church living in a very challenging world.

Thanks be to God, who gives hope for tomorrow!

| David Gilmore

Remember to follow through

2 Corinthians 8:2–7

> For during a severe ordeal of affliction, their abundant joy and their extreme poverty have overflowed in a wealth of generosity on their part. For, as I can testify, they voluntarily gave according to their means, and even beyond their means, begging us earnestly for the privilege of sharing in this ministry to the saints – and this, not merely as we expected; they gave themselves first to the Lord and, by the will of God, to us, so that we might urge Titus that, as he had already made a beginning, so he should also complete this generous undertaking among you. Now as you excel in everything – in faith, in speech, in knowledge, in utmost eagerness, and in our love for you – so we want you to excel also in this generous undertaking.
>
> (NRSV)

| David Gilmore

On occasion, I play golf and tennis. While I am far from accomplished in either sport, one lesson that I've heard in both is the importance of following through. Whether it is a tee shot in golf or a serve in tennis, to follow through prevents hooking, slicing and faulting. Following through is often the difference between success and failure in golf, in tennis and in life.

I took the circuitous route towards my degrees, because I allowed other things to distract me from completing my educational aspirations. This is a fancy way of saying that I did not follow through. It wasn't until I matured emotionally (and spiritually) that I was able to keep my eyes on the goal of graduation.

We do not know what 'afflictions' impacted the Macedonian faith community; however, their follow-through impacted Paul so much that he used them as an example of giving with gladness to the church at Corinth. The desire of the Macedonian faith community to engage in ministry was so great they sought out and found joy in giving in the midst of suffering.

How might life in our respective communities be better if we, the body of Christ, modelled our communal lives like that of Christ Jesus – with follow through? What would the perception of our neighbours be if we actually followed through, ensuring our actions and attitudes matched our words? I believe we might be viewed as 'straight shooters', rather than hooking on our intentions, slicing on our engagements and faulting on our promises.

Lord, help me to follow through for you.

| David Gilmore

Giving until it feels good

2 Corinthians 9:6–11

The point is this: the one who sows sparingly will also reap sparingly, and the one who sows bountifully will also reap bountifully. Each of you must give as you have made up your mind, not reluctantly or under compulsion, for God loves a cheerful giver. And God is able to provide you with every blessing in abundance, so that by always having enough of everything, you may share abundantly in every good work. As it is written, 'He scatters abroad, he gives to the poor; his righteousness endures forever.' He who supplies seed to the sower and bread for food will supply and multiply your seed for sowing and increase the harvest of your righteousness. You will be enriched in every way for your great generosity, which will produce thanksgiving to God through us.

(NRSV)

Reflection

Growing up in a Christian home in the US, I was taught at an early age that when the offering plate was passed around, I was supposed to put something in it. In fact, my grandmother would give me a nickel or dime to place in it. Now that I'm an adult, I can admit that I wanted to use my nickel or dime to buy candy. Later, I wanted to use my money in the clothing store or movie theatre rather than place it in an offering plate. You see, I didn't understand the significance of, or the theology in, my giving.

It was not until I had fallen away and then found my way back to church that I began to study the *why* behind giving. I don't give because of what I may receive in turn. This is not a quid pro quo relationship between the Lord and me, where I'm mistaking God for a cash machine, dating service or fortune teller. No, my giving is done with genuine gladness, because I'm reminded in these acts of what Christ gave for me. My giving is done with deep gratitude, because I know Jesus gave his all for me. There is no compunction or reticence in my giving, because the Lord has provided more than I could have imagined or deserved!

When I was a local church pastor, there was a rather cantankerous older gentleman who loudly asked me, 'Do you want to see me or my money?' I explained that I wanted to see both, but for different reasons. I wanted to see the man, because this was the means for us to enter into an authentic, trusting, loving relationship. I also wanted to see him giving, because this is an act of worship, or an encounter with the divine, where an authentic, trusting, loving relationship is being offered.

> How good do you feel when called to give? Remembering the sacrificial gift of Jesus should make us feel really good and grateful and generous in our giving.

Making lemonade

Philippians 4:4–7

Rejoice in the Lord always; again I will say, Rejoice. Let your gentleness be known to everyone. The Lord is near. Do not worry about anything, but in everything by prayer and supplication with thanksgiving let your requests be made known to God. And the peace of God, which surpasses all understanding, will guard your hearts and your minds in Christ Jesus.

(NRSV)

| David Gilmore

Reflection

In my family's home church, there was a time set aside for testimony. Every Sunday morning, my grandmother would stand and witness to how good God had been in hearing and responding to her prayers. For years I struggled hearing my grandmother's testimony, because I knew she barely had enough money to pay her bills or feed her family and she was facing significant life-threatening illnesses. How could she talk about how good God was, when nothing good seemed to be happening for her?

One day, I asked my grandmother about her strange-sounding testimonies, and she told me, 'Just because the world's given me lemons doesn't mean I can't make lemonade.' My grandmother's attitude took what could have been bitter and turned it into something sweet. Like Paul, she had learned not to worry. She may have been short of money, but the Lord allowed her to keep the lights on and the house heated. She may have been low on funds, but the Lord continually provided food for her and her family and her needy neighbours to eat. And she may have been sick in body, but the Lord had allowed her to see another day, which was more than some others.

I've learned that no matter how bad my life may seem, there is a reason for rejoicing, because I am here! No matter how adverse your circumstances may seem right now, you have a reason to rejoice, because you are alive to read or hear this reflection. This is my understanding of taking the world's lemons and allowing the Lord to make lemonade.

Make lemonade by praying for and with someone who needs to know that the Lord is near; by generously sharing your faith-filled, gentle spirit with everyone, believing that some will come to know the one who offers a peace 'which surpasses all understanding'.

> Lord, thank you that you are near. Today, may we make lemonade together.

David Gilmore

What really matters?

Philippians 4:10–14

I rejoice in the Lord greatly that now at last you have revived your concern for me; indeed, you were concerned for me, but had no opportunity to show it. Not that I am referring to being in need; for I have learned to be content with whatever I have. I know what it is to have little, and I know what it is to have plenty. In any and all circumstances I have learned the secret of being well-fed and of going hungry, of having plenty and of being in need. I can do all things through him who strengthens me. In any case, it was kind of you to share my distress.

(NRSV)

| David Gilmore

Reflection

As the director of congregational development and revitalisation for the New York Conference of the United Methodist Church, I have the often overwhelming responsibility of trying to effect positive change in an organisation that has experienced negative change for the past 35 years. Some days I have asked God aloud, 'Why, Lord, why?' What keeps me encouraged is that when I'm feeling at my lowest, the Lord dispatches angels to offer what I need. There have been many times when someone has texted or called to say, 'I just wanted you to know that I'm praying for you.' Or the Lord will send an 'angel' who will come by the office to take me to lunch or just to pray with me. I have been on the mountaintop and in the valley, and through it all the Lord keeps sending angels to minister to me.

In this text, Paul has been in both the penthouse and the outhouse, spreading this revolutionary message of God's unconditional love. He has been beaten, shipwrecked, struck blind and imprisoned. He has been revered and despised, blessed and cursed – sometimes by the same faith community. In his present circumstance, Paul is in a valley and is grateful for the unasked-for sharing of the church at Philippi. This is a faith community that isn't sharing in Paul's good times. This is a church that is gladly and generously sharing in Paul's distress.

How might lives be positively impacted by a faith community which intentionally shares in the distress of its neighbours? What kind of a trusting, loving fellowship might be fostered by a faith community who takes the time to see, hear and feel the pains, worries, fears and doubts of its neighbours? I would submit that what really matters to most is knowing that someone, anyone, is loving us when we are at our least.

Insurance or assurance?

1 Timothy 6:17–19

As for those who in the present age are rich, command them not to be haughty, or to set their hopes on the uncertainty of riches, but rather on God who richly provides us with everything for our enjoyment. They are to do good, to be rich in good works, generous, and ready to share, thus storing up for themselves the treasure of a good foundation for the future, so that they may take hold of the life that really is life.

(NRSV)

| David Gilmore

Reflection

My dictionary defines insurance as 'coverage by contract whereby one party undertakes to indemnify or guarantee another against loss by a specified contingency or peril'. I have life insurance, medical insurance, dental insurance, automobile and tyre insurance because I want to ensure that I and my family are protected.

The same rationale could be applied to how we view money. We believe that if we just save enough money, we will be assured a relaxed, stress-free retirement. Of course, the uncertainty of the stock markets and the determination of some governments to reduce or remove the promise of social security have some of us wondering if we can rely on a promise of an assured tomorrow. This uncertainty may cause us to worry about our future so much that we lose sight of those who are marginalised and ostracised.

As I have grown older (and hopefully wiser), what is becoming clearer is that I cannot do anything to ensure my future happiness. In our scriptures, Paul offers the advice to become rich in what we do rather than what we possess. Becoming 'rich in good works, generous, and ready to share' is what guarantees our future with the ultimate insurer, God. It is when we shift the focus from 'me' to 'we' that we have the assurance of a future with 'thee'! It is in this assurance that we can live a relaxed, assured life, knowing that the same God who provides for us today has ensured that we have an assured tomorrow, in a place where there is no stress, or contingency, or emergency, or hurt, or loneliness, or brokenness.

This type of assurance makes it much easier for me to offer radical generosity and share richly with my sisters and brothers who 'have not'. What about you?

| David Gilmore

What brings you joy?

1 John 1:1–4

> We declare to you what was from the beginning, what we have heard, what we have seen with our eyes, what we have looked at and touched with our hands, concerning the word of life – this life was revealed, and we have seen it and testify to it, and declare to you the eternal life that was with the Father and was revealed to us – we declare to you what we have seen and heard so that you also may have fellowship with us; and truly our fellowship is with the Father and with his Son Jesus Christ. We are writing these things so that our joy may be complete.
>
> (NRSV)

Reflection

What brings you joy? I mean, what is that special something that brings you *real* joy? I love desserts. I love cakes and cupcakes, pies and tarts, puddings and custards, ice cream and gelato. As a child, the rule in our home was no dessert if we did not eat all our food. I always ate all my food, because I *love* desserts!

What brings the writer of 1 John joy is sharing that he has heard, seen and touched a revealed future with the divine. This person is offering a heartfelt testimony to a life-changing revelation from the Lord that what is being encountered in the present is not what is promised in the future. In other words, the stuff of today will be a thing of the past tomorrow. This revelation is not a happiness that is temporarily satisfying. No, this revelation brings the writer into a joy-filled state that is sustaining and eternal. What an amazingly inexplicable mystery – to be filled with a joy that reminds us that we have a tomorrow with God our Father and his Son Jesus!

When we experience this level of intimacy with our God, we must share this experience with everyone we encounter. But it goes much deeper than just sharing. When we experience this kind of love, we will gladly share this love with everyone we encounter. Because we have had grace poured upon our lives without measure, we become grace-filled disciples who love the unlovables and hug the unhuggables. We gladly share, remembering those instances when it was only God's grace that kept us from harming and/or doing harm. We gladly share, remembering the joy we experienced when we realised that God has claimed us as his very own.

> What brings you joy? Are you willing to share it with others?

Whole-church resources

MISSIONAL DISCIPLESHIP RESOURCES FOR CHURCHES

INTRODUCTORY GUIDE
HOLYHABITS

BIBLICAL TEACHING
They devoted themselves to the apostles' teaching and to fellowship, to the breaking of bread and to prayer.
HOLYHABITS

FELLOWSHIP
They devoted themselves to the apostles' teaching and fellowship, to the breaking of bread and to prayer.
HOLYHABITS

BREAKING BREAD
They devoted themselves to the apostles' teaching and fellowship, to the breaking of bread and to prayer.
HOLYHABITS

PRAYER
They devoted themselves to the apostles' teaching and to fellowship, to the breaking of bread and to prayer.
HOLYHABITS

SHARING RESOURCES
All the believers were together and had everything in common.
HOLYHABITS

SERVING
All the believers were together and had everything in common; they sold property and possessions to give to anyone who had need.
HOLYHABITS

EATING TOGETHER
They broke bread in their homes and ate together with glad and sincere hearts, praising God and enjoying the favour of all the people.
HOLYHABITS

GLADNESS AND GENEROSITY
They broke bread in their homes and ate together with glad and sincere hearts, praising God and enjoying the favour of all the people.
HOLYHABITS

WORSHIP
They broke bread in their homes and ate together with glad and sincere hearts, praising God and enjoying the favour of all the people.
HOLYHABITS

MAKING MORE DISCIPLES
And the Lord added to their number daily those who were being saved.
HOLYHABITS

Individual copy £4.99

Holy Habits is an adventure in Christian discipleship. Inspired by Luke's model of church found in Acts 2:42–47, it identifies ten habits and encourages the development of a way of life formed by them. These resources are designed to help churches explore the habits creatively in a range of contexts and live them out in whole-life, intergenerational, missional discipleship.

HOLYHABITS

Original design by morsebrowndesign.co.uk & penguinboy.net

These new additions to the Holy Habits resources have been developed to help churches and individuals explore the Holy Habits through prayerful engagement with the Bible and live them out in whole-life, missional discipleship.

Bible Reflections Edited by Andrew Roberts | Individual copy £3.99

Each set of Bible reading notes contains eight weeks of devotional material. Four writers bring different perspectives on the habit in question through their reflections on passages drawn from across the Bible narrative.

Group Studies Edited by Andrew Roberts | Individual copy £6.99

Each leader's guide contains eight sessions of Bible study material, providing off-the-peg material to help churches get started or continue with Holy Habits. Each session includes a Bible passage, reflections, group questions, community/outreach ideas, art and media links and a prayer.

Find out more at **holyhabits.org.uk**
and **brfonline.org.uk/collections/holy-habits**
Download a leaflet for your church leadership at
brfonline.org.uk/holyhabitsdownload

Are you looking to continue the habit of daily Bible reading?

With a subscription to BRF Bible reading notes, you'll have everything you need to nourish your relationship with the Bible and with God.

Our most popular and longest running series, *New Daylight*, features daily readings and reflections from a selection of much-beloved writers, dealing with a variety of themes and Bible passages. With the relevant passage printed alongside the comment, *New Daylight* is a practical and effective way of reading the Bible as a part of your everyday routine.

New Daylight is available in print, deluxe (large print), by email and as an app for iOS and Android.

'I think Bible reading notes are really underrated. At any age – there I was as a teenager getting as much out of them then as I am now – so they're for every age group, not just the very young and the very old. I think to have them as your bedside companion is a really wise idea throughout life.'
Debbie Thrower, Pioneer of BRF's Anna Chaplaincy programme

Included in this issue
Genesis 37—45: Joseph AMANDA BLOOR
What hath God wrought! MURDO MACDONALD
Gardens in the Bible BARBARA MOSSE

Also available:

Find out more at brfonline.org.uk

Praise for the original Holy Habits resources

'Here are some varied and rich resources to help further deepen our discipleship of Christ, encouraging and enabling us to adopt the life-transforming habits that make for following Jesus.'
Revd Dr Martyn Atkins, Team Leader & Superintendent Minister, Methodist Central Hall, Westminster

'The Holy Habits resources will help you, your church, your fellowship group, to engage in a journey of discovery about what it really means to be a disciple today. I know you will be encouraged, challenged and inspired as you read and work your way through… There is lots to study together and pray about, and that can only be good as our churches today seek to bring about the kingdom of God.'
Revd Loraine Mellor, President of the Methodist Conference 2017/18

'The Holy Habits resources help weave the spiritual through everyday life. They're a great tool that just get better with use. They help us grow in our desire to follow Jesus as their concern is formation not simply information.'
Olive Fleming Drane and John Drane

'The Holy Habits resources are an insightful and comprehensive manual for living in the way of Jesus in the 21st century: an imaginative, faithful and practical gift for the church that will sustain and invigorate our life and mission in a demanding world. The Holy Habits resources are potentially transformational for a church.'
Revd Ian Adams, Mission Spirituality Adviser for Church Mission Society

'To understand the disciplines of the Christian life without practising them habitually is like owning a fine collection of soap but never having a wash. The team behind Holy Habits knows this, which is why they have produced these excellent and practical resources. Use them, and by God's grace you will grow in holiness.'
Paul Bayes, Bishop of Liverpool